Shapes

I See Triangles

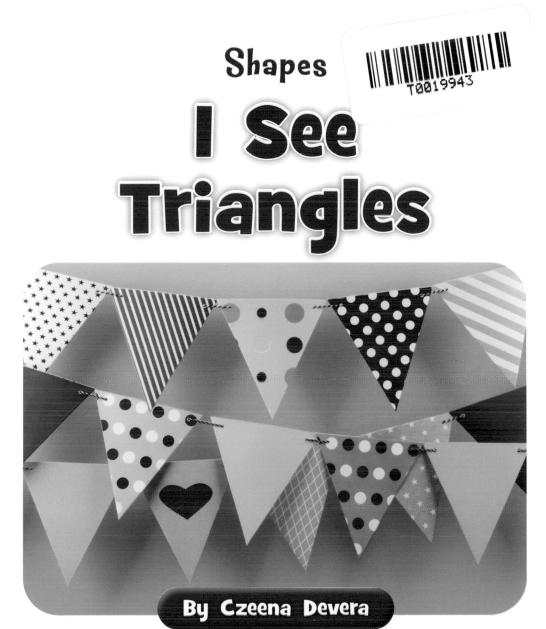

By Czeena Devera

2 There is one triangle.

There are two triangles.

There are three triangles.

There are four triangles.

There are five triangles.

There are six triangles.

There are seven triangles.

There are eight triangles.

There are nine triangles.

There are ten triangles.

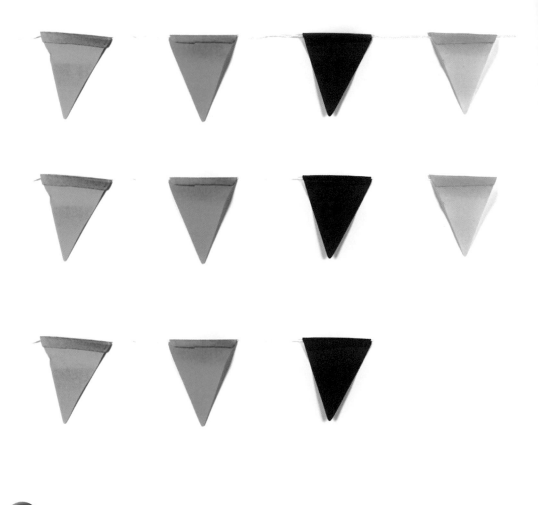

There are eleven triangles.

There are twelve triangles.

one	four	nine
triangle	five	ten
two	six	eleven
triangles	seven	twelve
three	eight	

There is one triangle.

There are two triangles.

There are three triangles.

There are four triangles.

There are five triangles.

There are six triangles.

There are seven triangles.

There are eight triangles.

There are nine triangles.

There are ten triangles.

There are eleven triangles.

There are twelve triangles.

CHERRY BLOSSOM PRESS

Published in the United States of America by Cherry Lake Publishing Group
Ann Arbor, Michigan
www.cherrylakepublishing.com

Photo Credits: © Didecs/Shutterstock.com, front cover, 1; © sportoakimirka/Shutterstock.com, 2;
© NIPAPORN PANYACHAROEN/Shutterstock.com, 3, 14; © Viktor1/Shutterstock.com, 4;
© Eshma/Shutterstock.com, 5; © Holiday.Photo.Top/Shutterstock.com, 6, back cover;
© Yeti studio/Shutterstock.com, 7; © Vagengeim/Shutterstock.com, 8; © YesPhotographers/
Shutterstock.com, 9, 13; © Kuki Ladron de Guevara/Shutterstock.com, 10; © Daria Medvedeva/
Shutterstock.com, 11; © Pao Laroid/Shutterstock.com, 12

Cherry Blossom Press is an imprint of Cherry Lake Publishing Group.

Library of Congress Cataloging-in-Publication Data

Names: Devera, Czeena, author.
Title: I see triangles / Czeena Devera.
Description: Ann Arbor, Michigan : Cherry Lake Publishing, 2021. | Series: Shapes | Audience:
Grades K-1 | Summary: "Spot triangles and count in this book. Beginning readers will gain confidence
with the Whole Language approach to literacy, a combination of sight words and repetition. Bold,
colorful photographs correlate directly to the text to help guide readers as they engage with the book"
— Provided by publisher.
Identifiers: LCCN 2020030261 (print) | LCCN 2020030262 (ebook) | ISBN
9781534179851 (paperback) | ISBN 9781534180864 (pdf) | ISBN 9781534182578 (ebook)
Subjects: LCSH: Triangle—Juvenile literature.
Classification: LCC QA482 .D485 2021 (print) | LCC QA482 (ebook) | DDC 516/.154—dc23
LC record available at https://lccn.loc.gov/2020030261
LC ebook record available at https://lccn.loc.gov/2020030262

Cherry Lake Publishing Group would like to acknowledge the work of the Partnership for 21st Century
Learning, a Network of Battelle for Kids. Please visit *http://www.battelleforkids.org/networks/p21*
for more information.

Printed in the United States of America
Corporate Graphics